DISCOVERING LANGUAGES
FRENCH

REVISED EDITION

Elaine S. Robbins

Formerly Mount Logan Middle School
Logan, Utah

Kathryn R. Ashworth

Brigham Young University

AMSCO SCHOOL PUBLICATIONS, INC.,
a division of Perfection Learning®

To the memory of

Carl C. Robbins Jr., beloved son and brother of the authors

Design and Production: Boultinghouse & Boultinghouse, Inc.

Cover Illustration: Delana Bettoli

Illustrations: Rick Brown, John R. Jones, Ed Taber, George Ulrick

ISBN 978-1-56765-333-5

© 2006, 1995 by Amsco School Publications, Inc.,
a division of Perfection Learning®

Please visit our website at:
www.amscopub.com and *www.perfectionlearning.com*

When ordering this book, please specify:
ISBN 978-1-56765-333-5 or **1349501**

9 10 11 12 13 14   DR   24 23 22 21 20 19

Printed in the United States of America

To the Student

You are about to embark on a journey of discovery — beginning to learn a new language spoken by millions of people around the world, FRENCH.

Learning French provides an opportunity to explore another language and culture. French may be one of several languages you will discover in this course. You can then select which language you will continue to study.

Whatever your goals, this book will be a fun beginning in exploring a special gift you have as a human being: the ability to speak a language other than your own. The more you learn how to communicate with other people, the better you will be able to live and work in the world around you.

In this book, you will discover the French language and the world where it is spoken. The French words and expressions you will learn have been limited so that you will feel at ease.

You will learn how to express many things in French: how to greet people, how to count, how to tell the day and month of the year, how to identify and describe many objects, and more.

You will use French to talk about yourself and your friends. You will practice with many different activities, like puzzles and word games, French songs, cartoons, and pictures. Some activities you will do with classmates or with the whole class. You will act out fun skits and conversations and sing French songs. You will learn about many interesting bits of French culture: school days, holidays, leisure time, name days, gestures, and sports.

You will also meet young Claude, who will be your guide on how to pronounce French words. Look for Claude's clues throughout this book and get a feel for the French language, its sounds, and its musical quality. You will also develop an ear for French, so listen carefully to your teacher and the cassettes.

You will quickly realize that learning a new language is not as hard as you might have imagined. Enjoy using it with your teacher and classmates. Try not to be shy or afraid of making mistakes when speaking: remember, the more you speak, the more you will learn. And you can even show off the French you learn to family, relatives, and friends. After all, learning a new language means talking with the rest of the world and with each other.

Now — on to French. **Bonne chance!**, which means *Good luck!*

— *K.R.A.*

Contents

France and the French Language

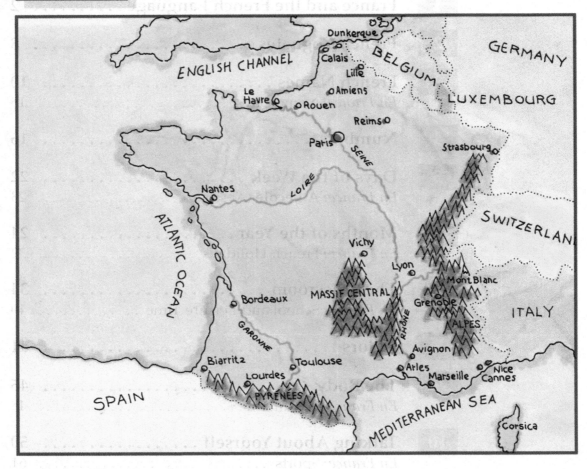

France, slightly smaller than the state of Texas, is the largest country in western Europe. Situated at the western edge of the European continent, France is shaped roughly like a hexagon, a six-sided figure. In fact, the French refer to their country as **l'hexagone**. Three of its sides border on water: the Mediterranean Sea, the Atlantic Ocean, and the English Channel. The other three sides border on land: Spain, Italy, Switzerland, Germany, Luxembourg, and Belgium.

The geography of France is varied, with low-lying plains, plateaus, forests, and mountains. Europe's highest peak, Mont Blanc, is located in southeastern France. The country is crisscrossed by four major river systems and their interconnecting canals. As an important agricultural center, France produces most of the foods its people consume.

France, often called **"la douce France"** (sweet France), was formerly a great colonial power. Its explorers and traders took the French language to many parts of the world. Paris, called **"la ville-lumière"** (the city of light), is the capital of France and one of the world's most beautiful cities.

The French language, derived from Latin, is a Romance language, like Spanish, Italian, Portuguese, and Romanian. Written in the Roman alphabet, French belongs to the Indo-European family of languages. The letters are the same as those in the English alphabet, but they are pronounced much differently. For example, the word Paris, written the same in English, is pronounced without the final **s** sound. There are also many accent marks in French that affect the sounds and/or the meanings of words.

French is the official language of more than twenty countries around the world. Over one hundred and twenty million people speak French as their native language. In Europe, outside of France, French is spoken in Belgium, Luxembourg, Switzerland, and Monaco. On the American continent, French is the official language of three islands in the Caribbean: Haiti, Martinique, and Guadeloupe. Quebec, Canada's largest province, is almost entirely French-speaking. In the United States, French is a second language for more than a million people in Louisiana and certain areas of Vermont, New Hampshire, and Maine.

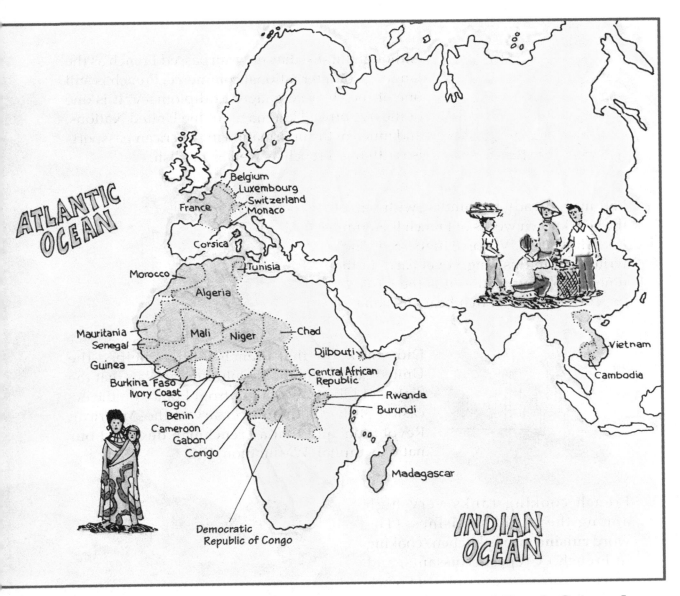

In South America, French is the official language of French Guiana. In Africa, France built a great colonial empire toward the end of the nineteenth century. French is still the official or second language in many African countries that were once French colonies: Algeria, Tunisia, Morocco, Senegal, Cameroon, Zaire, the Ivory Coast, and several other countries. These countries retain not only the French language but also the influence of French culture, institutions, and traditions. In Asia, the countries of Laos, Cambodia, and Vietnam (formerly Indochina) were also at one time French colonies, and French is still spoken today by some of their people.

Although English has now surpassed French as the language of international commerce, French is still one of the chief languages of diplomacy. It is one of the five official languages of the United Nations, and much of the information in American passports is written in French as well as English.

You may already be familiar with one of the best-known works of French literature, *Les Misérables*. Victor Hugo, a French writer, wrote this long novel early in the nineteenth century, and it is the basis for the current musical that bears its name.

Did you know that French soldiers helped the United States win the Revolutionary War, that the Statue of Liberty was a gift from France on the occasion of the 100th anniversary of the American Revolution, and that a Frenchman designed our nation's capital, Washington, D.C.?

French cooking ranks very high among the world's cuisines. (The word **cuisine** means kitchen/cooking in French.) Crêpes, croissants, and omelettes are tasty examples of French food. Many English food words come from French: **mouton** = *mutton*, **bœuf** = *beef*, and **porc** = *pork*.

Now you have the opportunity to study this beautiful and influential language. Have fun and enjoy it.

1. How does France compare with other European countries in size?

   _____

2. Name the Romance languages.

   _____

3. Where is the highest mountain in Europe?

   _____

4. How many countries retain French as their official language?

   _____

5. How many people throughout the world speak French as their native

   language? _____

6. What two languages are on American passports?

   _____

7. Name three islands in the Caribbean where French is spoken.

   _____

8. Can you name two French foods?

   _____

9. Which continent has the greatest number of French-speaking countries?

   _____

10. Who wrote the novel entitled *Les Misérables*? _____

11. What do the Statue of Liberty and croissants have in common?

   _____

2 French Cognates

You already know many French words. Some of the words are spelled exactly like English words. In many other words, the only difference between English and French is an accent mark on one or two letters. One clue to watch for is the circumflex accent, which often occurs in a French word over a vowel that in English is followed by *s*: **hôpital** = *hospital*, **forêt** = *forest*. Also, words ending in *-er* in English frequently end in **-re** in French: **centre** = *center*, **décembre** = *December*. Words ending in *-y* in English often end in **-é** in French: **nationalité** = *nationality*, **réalité** = *reality*.

How many of the following French words can you recognize? Fill in the blanks with the English meanings. If you need to, you may look in a dictionary. Listen to your teacher or the cassette for the pronunciation of these words:

1. aéroport _airport_
2. américain _america_
3. ancêtre _answer_
4. appartement _apartment_
5. armée _army_
6. arriver _river_
7. art _art_
8. autobus _bus_
9. automobile _car_
10. banane _banana_

11. bleu _blue_
12. carotte _carrot_
13. centre _center_
14. céréale _cereal_
15. certainement _entertainment_
16. charmant _?_
17. chocolat _chocolate_
18. classe _class_
19. décembre _december_
20. dîner _dinner_

21. électricien _electrician_

22. famille _family_

23. géographie _geography_

24. histoire _history_

25. hôpital _hospital_

26. hôtel _hotel_

27. idéal _ideal_

28. imaginer _imagine_

29. lion _lion_

30. liberté _libray_

31. mai _me_

32. maman _mom_

33. moderne _modern_

34. modèle _model_

35. musique _music_

36. national _natioal_

37. nationalité _nationally_

38. oncle _uncle_

39. personne _person_

40. poème _poem_

41. poète _poet_

42. problème _problem_

43. réalité _reality_

44. salade _salad_

45. sandale _sandal_

46. théâtre _theater_

47. tigre _tiger_

48. timide _timid_

49. touriste _tourist_

50. visite _visit_

3 French Names

Now that you are able to recognize over 50 French words resembling English, let's look at how French and English names compare.

Claude is going to help you learn how to pronounce some of these names.

You will meet **Claude** throughout this book holding his lens over one or two pronunciation clues he wants to share with you as you develop a good French pronunciation.

Whenever you look at **Claude**'s clues, keep this in mind: every time you try to pronounce a French sound, hold your mouth, tongue, lips, and teeth in the same position at the end of the sound as you did at the beginning. Try saying **o** this way. Now try **oooo**. There, you've got it.

Claude has two clues for you before you listen to the following list of boys' and girls' names. These clues tell you how to pronounce HIS name:

Pauline, Claudine

Claude, Marie

Here is a list of boys' and girls' names. With your teacher's help, choose a French name that you would like to have for yourself while you are studying French:

Alain	Frédéric	Grégoire	Jacques	Laurent
Albert	Georges	Guillaume	Jean	Léon
Alexandre				Marc
André				Marcel
Antoine				Michel
Bernard				Nicolas
Bruno				Olivier
Charles				Paul
Claude				Philippe
Denis				Pierre
Didier				Raoul
Dominique				Raymond
Édouard				René
Étienne	Gérard	Guy	Joseph	Vincent
François	Gilbert	Henri	Julien	Yves

Adèle	Françoise	Isabelle	Madeleine	Michèle
Anne	Gabrielle	Jacqueline	Marguerite	Monique
Antoinette				Nathalie
Béatrice				Nicole
Bernadette				Patricia
Blanche				Pauline
Brigitte				Simone
Catherine				Solange
Cécile				Sophie
Chantal				Suzanne
Claire				Suzette
Claudine				Sylvie
Colette				Thérèse
Dominique				Véronique
Dorothée				Virginie
Élisabeth	Geneviève	Jeanne	Marie	Yolande
Estelle	Hélène	Lise	Marthe	Yvette

When the French want to say, "My name is Marie," they say, **"Je m'appelle Marie."** Practice telling your teacher and your classmates your name in French. For instance, "Je m'appelle Robert." If you and your teacher have chosen French names, use them.

Je m'appelle Marie.

Claude's clues:

ç = s

The **n** of the nasal sound is not pronounced.

vowel + **n** or **m** may be nasal.

Ça va?

France, enchanté, Vincent, bonjour, lundi

* **tu** means *you* in French; **tu** is used when you are speaking to a close relative, a friend, or a child — someone with whom you are familiar. To say *you*, the French also use **vous** when speaking to a stranger or a grown-up — a person with whom you should be formal. The exercises in this book use **tu** and its related forms **toi** and **te** (**t'**).

Now let's review what you learned in Dialog 1:

1. Bonjour, _____ (name).

Bonjour, _____ (name).

2. Comment t'appelles-tu?

Je m'appelle _____.

3. Enchanté, _____ (name).

Enchantée,* _____ (name).

4. Au revoir.

Au revoir.

---

* Did you notice in Dialog 1 that Pierre says **Enchanté** and Solange says **Enchantée**? The reason is that French nouns and adjectives, unlike English, have gender. They are either masculine or feminine. An **e** is often added to the masculine form to make it feminine.

JANVIER	FÉVRIER	MARS	AVRIL
1 J. de L'AN	1 sᵉ Ella	1 s Aubin	1 s Hugues
2 s Basile	2 **Présentation**	2 s Ch. le Bon	2 sᵉ Sandrine
3 sᵉ Geneviève	3 s Blaise	3 s Guénolé	3 s Richard
4 s Odilon	4 sᵉ Véronique	4 **Carême**	4 s Isidore
5 s Édouard	5 sᵉ Agathe	5 sᵉ Olive	5 sᵉ Irène
6 s Melaine	6 s Gaston	6 sᵉ Colette	6 s Marcellin
7 **Épiphanie**	7 sᵉ Eugénie	7 sᵉ Félicité	7 s J.B. de la S.
8 s Lucien	8 sᵉ Jacqueline	8 s Jean de D.	8 **Rameaux**
9 sᵉ Alix	9 sᵉ Apolline	9 sᵉ Franç R.	9 s Gautier
10 s Guillaume	10 s Arnaud	10 s Vivien	10 s Fulbert
11 s Paulin	11 N.-D. Lourdes	11 sᵉ Rosine	11 s Stanislas
12 sᵉ Tatiana	12 s Félix	12 sᵉ Justine	12 s Jules
13 sᵉ Yvette	13 sᵉ Béatrice	13 s Rodrigue	13 **Vend. Saint**
14 sᵉ Nina	14 s Valentin	14 sᵉ Mathilde	14 s Maxime
15 s Remi	15 s Claude	15 sᵉ Louise M.	15 **PÂQUES**
16 s Marcel	16 sᵉ Julienne	16 sᵉ Bénédicte	16 s Ben. J. L.
17 sᵉ Roseline	17 s Alexis	17 s Patrice	17 s Anicet
18 sᵉ Prisca	18 sᵉ Bernadette	18 s Cyrille	18 s Parfait
19 s Marius	19 s Gabin	19 s Joseph	19 sᵉ Emma
20 s Sébastien	20 sᵉ Aimée	20 s Herbert	20 sᵉ Odette
21 sᵉ Agnès	21 s P. Damien	21 sᵉ Clémence	21 s Anselme
22 s Vincent	22 sᵉ Isabelle	22 **Mi-Carême**	22 s Alexandre
23 s Barnard	23 s Lazare	23 s Victorien	23 s Georges
24 s Franç. Sales	24 s Modeste	24 **Annonciat.**	24 s Fidèle
25 Conv. s. Paul	25 s Roméo	25 s Humbert	25 s Marc
26 sᵉ Paule	26 s Nestor	26 sᵉ Larissa	26 sᵉ Alida
27 sᵉ Angèle	27 **Mardi gras**	27 s Habib	27 sᵉ Zita
28 s Th. D'Aquin	28 **Cendres**	28 s Gontran	28 sᵉ Valérie
29 s Gildas		29 sᵉ Gwladys	29 **Souvenir Dép.**
30 sᵉ Martine		30 s Amédée	30 s Robert
31 sᵉ Marcelle		31 s Benjamin	

MAI	JUIN	JUILLET	AOÛT
1 **TRAVAIL**	1 s Justin	1 s Thierry	1 s Alphonse
2 s Boris	2 sᵉ Blandine	2 s Martin	2 s Julien
3 ss Phil./Jacq.	3 **PENTECÔTE**	3 s Thomas	3 sᵉ Lydie
4 s Sylvain	4 sᵉ Clotilde	4 s Florent	4 s JM Vianney
5 sᵉ Judith	5 s Igor	5 s Ant.-Marie	5 s Abel
6 sᵉ Prudence	6 s Norbert	6 sᵉ Marietta G.	6 **Transfig.**
7 sᵉ Gisèle	7 s Gilbert	7 s Raoul	7 s Gaétan
8 **Victoire 1945**	8 s Médard	8 s Thibaut	8 s Dominique
9 s Pacôme	9 sᵉ Diane	9 sᵉ Amand.	9 s Amour
10 sᵉ Solange	10 s Landry	10 s Ulrich	10 s Laurent
11 sᵉ Estelle	11 s Barnabé	11 s Benoît	11 sᵉ Claire
12 s Achille	12 s Guy	12 s Olivier	12 sᵉ Clarisse
13 **Fête J. d'Arc**	13 s Ant. de Pa.	13 ss Henri/Joël	13 s Hippol.
14 s Matthias	14 s Élisée	14 **FÊTE NAT.**	14 s Evrard
15 sᵉ Denise	15 sᵉ Germaine	15 s Donald	15 **ASSOMPT.**
16 s Honoré	16 s J.F. Régis	16 ND Mt. Car.	16 s Armel
17 s Pascal	17 s Hervé	17 sᵉ Charlotte	17 s Hyacinthe
18 s Éric	18 s Léonce	18 s Frédéric	18 sᵉ Hélène
19 s Yves	19 s Romuald	19 s Arsène	19 s Jean Eudes
20 s Bernardin	20 s Silvère	20 sᵉ Marina	20 s Bernard
21 s Constant.	21 s Rudolphe	21 s Victor	21 s Christophe
22 s Émile	22 **Sacré-Coeur**	22 sᵉ Marie-Mad.	22 s Fabrice
23 s Didier	23 sᵉ Audrey	23 sᵉ Brigitte	23 sᵉ Rose
24 **ASCENSION**	24 s Jean-Bapt.	24 sᵉ Christine	24 s Barthélemy
25 sᵉ Sophie	25 s Prosper	25 s Jac. le Maj.	25 s Louis
26 s Bérenger	26 s Anthelme	26 sᵉ Anne	26 sᵉ Natache
27 **F. des Mères**	27 s Fernand	27 sᵉ Nathalie	27 sᵉ Monique
28 s Germain	28 s Irénée	28 s Samson	28 s Augustin
29 s Aymar	29 ss Pierre/Paul	29 sᵉ Marthe	29 sᵉ Sabine
30 s Ferdinand	30 s Martial	30 sᵉ Juliette	30 s Fiacre
31 **Visitation**		31 s Ignace de L.	31 s Aristide

SEPTEMBRE	OCTOBRE	NOVEMBRE	DÉCEMBRE
1 s Gilles	1 sᵉ Thér. EJ	1 **TOUSSAINT**	1 sᵉ Florence
2 sᵉ Ingrid	2 s Léger	2 **Défunts**	2 **Avent**
3 s Grégoire	3 s Gérard	3 s Hubert	3 s Fr.-Xavier
4 sᵉ Rosalie	4 s Franç. d'As.	4 s Charles Bo.	4 sᵉ Barbara
5 sᵉ Raissa	5 sᵉ Fleur	5 sᵉ Sylvie	5 s Gérald
6 s Bertrand	6 s Bruno	6 sᵉ Bertille	6 s Nicolas
7 sᵉ Reine	7 s Serge	7 sᵉ Carine	7 s Ambroise
8 **Nativité N-D**	8 sᵉ Pélagie	8 s Geoffroy	8 **Imm. Conc.**
9 s Alain	9 s Denis	9 s Théodore	9 s P. Fourier
10 sᵉ Inès	10 s Ghislain	10 s Léon	10 s Romaric
11 s Adelphe	11 s Firmin	11 **Vict. 1918**	11 s Daniel
12 s Apollinaire	12 s Wilfried	12 s Christian	12 s JF de Chant.
13 s Aimé	13 s Géraud	13 s Brice	13 sᵉ Lucie
14 **Sainte Croix**	14 s Juste	14 s Sidoine	14 sᵉ Odile
15 s Roland	15 sᵉ Thér. A	15 s Albert	15 sᵉ Ninon
16 sᵉ Édith	16 sᵉ Edwige	16 sᵉ Marguerite	16 sᵉ Alice
17 s Renaud	17 s Baudouin	17 sᵉ Elisabeth	17 s Judicaël
18 sᵉ Nadège	18 s Luc	18 sᵉ Aude	18 s Gatien
19 sᵉ Émilie	19 s René	19 s Tanguy	19 s Urbain
20 s Davy	20 sᵉ Adeline	20 s Edmond	20 s Théophile
21 s Matthieu	21 sᵉ Céline	21 **Présent. N-D**	21 s P. Canisius
22 s Maurice	22 sᵉ Salomé	22 sᵉ Cécile	22 sᵉ Fr.-Xavière
23 s Constant	23 s Jean de Ca.	23 s Clément	23 s Armand
24 sᵉ Thècle	24 s Florentin	24 sᵉ Flora	24 sᵉ Adèle
25 s Hermann	25 s Crépin	25 sᵉ Cath. Lab.	25 **NOËL**
26 ss Côme/Dam.	26 s Dimitri	26 sᵉ Delphine	26 s Étienne
27 s Vinc. de P.	27 sᵉ Émeline	27 s Séverin	27 s Jean Apôt.
28 s Venceslas	28 s Simon	28 s Jacq. de M.	28 ss Innocents
29 s Michel	29 s Narcisse	29 s Saturnin	29 s David
30 s Jérôme	30 sᵉ Bienvenue	30 s André	30 **Ste Famille**
	31 s Quentin		31 s Sylvestre

En France

Name Days

All children look forward to their special day, their birthday. French children are doubly lucky. They celebrate not only their birthday but also their name day. Most French names come from the names of saints. If you look at a French calendar, you will notice that each day is devoted to a different saint. For example, if your name is Nathalie, your name day is July 27. On their name day, French children may receive presents and celebrate at an afternoon party with friends or at a special dinner with family. Everyone wishes them **Bonne Fête** (*Happy Name Day!*)

When children become adults, more importance is given to celebrating name days than birthdays. Cards and flowers are always offered as presents and everyone knows when to wish you **Bonne Fête!**

4 Numbers

Claude's clues:

r = almost a gargle

French **r** is pronounced at the back of the throat almost like a gargle.

é et final er } = eh

tigre, liberté   enchanté, aéroport, Olivier, et

You will soon be able to count to forty in French.
Listen to your teacher or the cassette to learn how
to say the numbers 1 to 20.

1 un 2 deux 3 trois 4 quatre 5 cinq 6 six
7 sept 8 huit 9 neuf 10 dix 11 onze 12 douze 13 treize
14 quatorze 15 quinze 16 seize 17 dix-sept 18 dix-huit 19 dix-neuf 20 vingt

ACTIVITÉ

1. Cover page 16 with a sheet of paper. Then cover the French number words below and say the numbers aloud in French.
2. Now cover the French number words and write the French number words in the blank lines.

onze	_____1_____	11	trois	_____	3
dix-huit	____16____	18	huit	_____	8
quinze	____15____	15	un	_____	1
cinq	_____	5	quatorze	_____	14
douze	_____	12	six	_____	6
sept	_____	7	deux	_____	2
dix-neuf	_____	19	neuf	_____	9
dix	_____	10	treize	_____	13
vingt	_____	20	seize	_____	16
quatre	_____	4	dix-sept	_____	17

3. Pretend you are the teacher and correct your work with a red pen or pencil. You will be able to see at a glance which words you need to study further.

ACTIVITÉ

Your teacher will read some French numbers to you. Write the numerals for the number you hear:

1. _____   4. _____   7. _____   10. _____

2. _____   5. _____   8. _____   11. _____

3. _____   6. _____   9. _____   12. _____

Let's continue learning numbers. Listen to your teacher or the cassette to learn how to say the numbers 21 to 40.

ACTIVITÉ

Cover the top of this page with a sheet of paper while you do the next three activities. Your teacher will read some numbers from 21 to 40 to you in random order. Write the numerals for the French number you hear.

1. _____

2. _____

3. _____

4. _____

5. _____

6. _____

7. _____

8. _____

9. _____

10. _____

See how many French number words you can recognize. Draw a line to match the French number word with its numeral:

vingt-six	40
trente-deux	34
vingt-trois	21
trente-quatre	36
vingt-neuf	23
quarante	28
trente-six	32
vingt-huit	39
trente-neuf	26
vingt et un	29

ACTIVITÉ

Now your teacher will read some numbers in English. Write the number words in French:

1. _____   6. _____

2. _____   7. _____

3. _____   8. _____

4. _____   9. _____

5. _____   10. _____

Now that you know the numbers from 1 to 40, let's try some math. First let's look at some other words you will need to know:

Now write the answers to the following arithmetic problems in French. Then find the correct answers in the puzzle. Circle them from left to right, right to left, up or down, or diagonally:

1. trente-deux moins vingt-deux font _____ dix

2. dix-neuf moins deux font _____ dix sept

3. neuf et sept font _____ seize

4. quinze et quinze font _____ trente

5. vingt et vingt font _____ quarante

6. onze moins sept font _____ quatre

7. quatorze moins deux font _____ douze

8. vingt-deux et trois font _____ dix -nuhf

9. trente-huit moins vingt font _____ dix - huit

10. vingt-sept et douze font _____ vingt- neuf

11. quinze et cinq font _____ vingt

12. sept et sept font _____ quatorze

13. vingt-trois moins huit font   _quinze_

14. sept et six font   _treize_

15. sept et vingt-quatre font   _trente - un_

16. douze moins cinq font   _sept_

17. vingt-six et sept font   _trente-trois_

18. quarante moins dix-neuf font   _vingt - un_
     40-19

19. seize moins cinq font   _neuf_

20. vingt-six moins sept font   _dix - neuf_
     26 - 7

```
I V I N G T C I N Q F U E E
L I A Q U A R A N T E I X Z
T N Z M Z Q U A T R E D D R
I G D D O P F Q S E F I H O
U T C R F N A H U X X X A T
H Y D I X S E P T N L K R A
X N U T E E T N E R T E M U
I E Z I E S S U E Z N I U Q
D U Q R A I F Q X T D N D E
N O G L F U E N E T N E R T
P N P Z A H C I Q G S R X I
E Z U O D V I N G T E T U N
K E Z I E R T K L N P O R U
S I O R T E T N E R T Y A X
```

5 Days of the Week

Claude's clues:

a alone
= ah

mardi, samedi

i alone
= ee
of meet

jeudi, vendredi

NOVEMBRE

lundi	mardi	mercredi	jeudi	vendredi	samedi	dimanche
1	2	3	4	5	6	7
8	9	10	11	12	13	14
15	16	17	18	19	20	21
22	23	24	25	26	27	28
29	30	31				

These are the days of the week in French. The first letter is not capitalized. The French week begins with Monday.

C'est aujourd'hui lundi. = *Today is Monday.*

Each day, find as many people as you can and tell them the day of the week in French, and write it down, too.

À l'école (At school)

Complete the following school schedule with the subjects you are taking this year:

	LUNDI	MARDI	MERCREDI	JEUDI	VENDREDI

Now look at a schedule of a French middle-school student. Compare it with yours. What are the differences? What are the similarities?

	LUNDI	MARDI	MERCREDI	JEUDI	VENDREDI	SAMEDI
8:00 – 9:00	Math	French	French	English	Math	French
9:00 – 10:00	Civics	Science	Readings from students' journals	French	History	Physical Education
10:00 – 10:30	Recreation	English	Music	Recreation	Recreation	Drawing
10:30 – 11:00	Drawing	Recreation	English	Geography	Library	English
11:00 – 12:00	French	History		Math	Science	
2:00 – 3:00	Technology	Physical Education		Chemistry	Music	
3:00 – 4:00	Class trip to mountain-climbing center	French		Civics	French	
4:00 – 5:00		Robotics		Chess Club		

School is taken very seriously in France. Many students do not finish their classes until 4, 5, or 6 o'clock in the evening, except on Wednesday and Saturday, when they have a half-day.

French report cards are distributed three times a year. Grades range from 1 to 20, with 10 being the passing grade and 15 or more a very good grade.

Parents of French students receive weekly reports on the progress of their children. Teachers and parents may write notes, information, questions, and comments to each other in a special notebook of correspondence that all students keep.

6 Months of the Year

Claude's clues:

eu = uh

bleu, jeudi, monsieur

ille = ee-yuh

famille, juillet

The months of the year in French resemble English. Can you recognize all of them?

JANVIER

FÉVRIER

MARS

AVRIL

MAI

JUIN

JUILLET

AOÛT

SEPTEMBRE

OCTOBRE

NOVEMBRE

DÉCEMBRE

Unscramble the letters to form the name of a French month:

1. R R E E V F I

2. R L A I V

3. A I M

4. U J N I

5. B E C E D R M E

6. A S M R

7. T E S M P R E B E

8. R E J I V A N

9. L J E L U I T

10. O E E R N M V B

11. O T U A

12. T B C R O O E

Match the names of the months with their numbers by drawing lines between the two columns. For example, January is number one and December is number twelve:

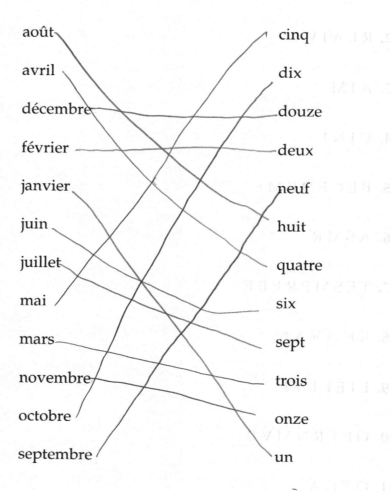

août	cinq
avril	dix
décembre	douze
février	deux
janvier	neuf
juin	huit
juillet	quatre
mai	six
mars	sept
novembre	trois
octobre	onze
septembre	un

Answer the following questions with the French months:

1. Which is your favorite month?

   Fevrier

2. Which is your least favorite month?

   Decembre

3. In which month is your birthday?

   Fevrier

4. In which month does your mother celebrate her birthday?

   a oût

5. In which month does your father celebrate his birthday?

   mai

6. In which month does your best friend celebrate her/his birthday?

   juillet

7. When does your teacher celebrate her / his birthday?

   Janvier

8. In which months do you have vacation?

   Juin, Julliet, Aout

9. In which month do maples turn red?

   fall _ septembre, Octobre, novembre

10. In which month do we fly kites?

    Mars, Avril

Fill in the blanks with the correct French names of the days or months, then find the nineteen names of the day or month in the puzzle. Circle them from left to right, right to left, up or down, or diagonally:

1. The first day of the week in France: _Lundi_

2. Many people go to church on this day of the week: _Samedi Dimanche_

3. The day after Monday: _Mardi_

4. The last day of your school week: _Vendredi_

5. The day after Tuesday: _Mercredi_

6. The first day of the weekend: _Samedi_

7. The next to the last day of your school week: _Jeudi_

8. The month of Valentine's Day: _Vendredi, Fevrier_

9. Flag Day is celebrated in this month: _Dimanche, June_

10. The first day of the new school year usually occurs in this month: _Lundi, Aout_

11. The month of Thanksgiving: _Jeudi, Novembre_

12. April Fool's Day is the first day of this month: _Mercredi, Avril_

13. The month of Christmas: _Vendredi, Decembre_

14. The month of the United States' birthday: _Samedi, Julliet_

15. The month after July: _Aout_

16. Memorial Day occurs toward the end of this month: _Lundi, mai_

17. Halloween is on the last day of this month: _Samedi , Octobre_

18. New Year's Day is the first day of this month: _vendredi, Janvier_

19. The month of St. Patrick's day: _mardi, Mars_

```
S E P T E M B R E A E R U Y U
W A X G G I W I J D V R F T H
U T N B X A M Q U Z I D A K J
O E S S A M E D I B E D S C E
H L C V G G I H N I P F J L U
O L R Y H M N O V E M B R E D
J I Z M A R S M E R C R E D I
L U K N F M K A O U T R S D O
A J C L D J B R Q M C N E T C
I H Y C N A P D B D F R Q N T
E F H L U N D I K L D E X M O
Z P N Y J V T X S N P T L P B
V O I R Q I K F E V R I E R R
W A L J Y E Y V U O Z B G O E
M G C A E R W D E C E M B R E
```

1=premier   ce   le

day # month

Now that you have learned the names of the days and months, let's learn how to say dates. When the French want to say, "Today is Monday, July fourteenth," they say, **"C'est aujourd'hui lundi, le quatorze juillet."** "Today is Friday, March first" would be **"C'est aujourd'hui vendredi, le premier* mars."**

Your teacher will divide the class into small groups. Each of you will choose your birthday month and make up a calendar for that month. Complete the calendar with the days of the week and the month in French and enter the dates.

LUNDI						DIMANCHE

Now that you have completed your calendar, take turns pointing to several dates and saying them to your partners. Then point to the date of your birthdate and say: **Mon anniversaire est** (*My birthday is*) . . . followed by the date.

---

* The French use the word **premier** instead of **un** for the first day of the month. **Premier** is easy to remember because it is a cognate; when you go to a movie's *premiere*, you go to its *first* performance.

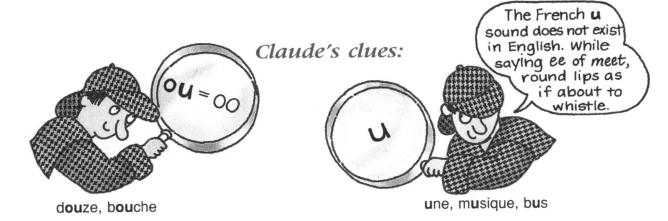

Claude's clues:

ou = oo

douze, bouche

The French **u** sound does not exist in English. While saying ee of meet, round lips as if about to whistle.

une, musique, bus

Dialog 2   *Qu'est-ce que c'est?*

Salut, Pierre.

Salut, Solange. Ça va?

Oui, ça va bien. Et toi?

Comme ci, comme ça.

Qu'est-ce que c'est?

C'est une fille.

Qu'est-ce que c'est?

C'est un soda pour toi.

Merci.

De rien.

ACTIVITÉ

Now let's review what you learned in Dialog 2:

1. Salut, _____Pierre_____ (name of friend). Ça va?

2. Comme ci, comme ça, et toi?
   Ça va bien.

3. Qu'est-ce que c'est?
   C'est un(e) _____fille_____.

4. Merci beaucoup.
   De rien.

En France **French Holidays**

What is the first thing many students look for on the school calendar? Days off. French students are given time off for the following holidays:

All Saints' Day (la Toussaint): November 1. A day in celebration of the saints and a day of remembrance of relatives and friends who have passed on. The week of All Saints' Day is a week of recess for French students.

Armistice Day (l'Armistice): November 11. The day that commemorates the end of World War I in 1918.

Christmas (Noël): December 25. Christmas Eve is celebrated with a midnight mass and a big dinner afterward. Children put shoes under the Christmas tree. During the night, Santa Claus (le père Noël) puts presents into the shoes. Students enjoy two weeks vacation during Christmas and New Year.

Winter Vacation. Students have a one-week recess in February.

Good Friday (le Vendredi Saint) and **Easter (Pâques).** Sugar eggs and chocolate are given to children.

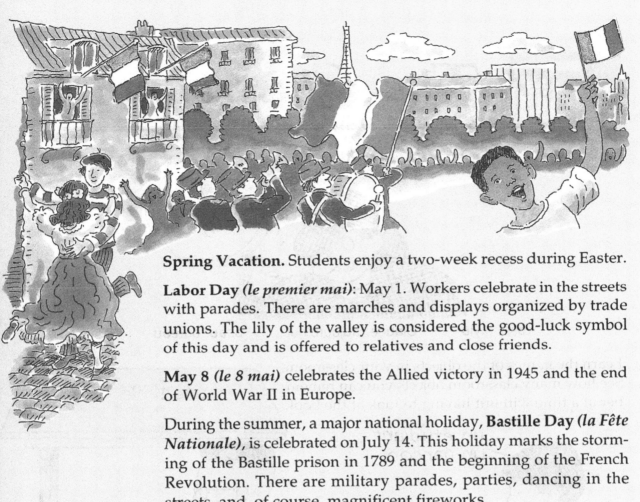

Spring Vacation. Students enjoy a two-week recess during Easter.

Labor Day (*le premier mai*): May 1. Workers celebrate in the streets with parades. There are marches and displays organized by trade unions. The lily of the valley is considered the good-luck symbol of this day and is offered to relatives and close friends.

May 8 (*le 8 mai*) celebrates the Allied victory in 1945 and the end of World War II in Europe.

During the summer, a major national holiday, **Bastille Day (*la Fête Nationale*)**, is celebrated on July 14. This holiday marks the storming of the Bastille prison in 1789 and the beginning of the French Revolution. There are military parades, parties, dancing in the streets, and, of course, magnificent fireworks.

Assumption Day (*l'Assomption*): August 15 is a very important summer holiday. In many towns there are religious processions and folklore festivals.

1. What is the name of the holiday on November 11 in the United States? <u>Veterans Day</u>

2. Which American holiday would you compare to **Bastille Day**?
<u>July 4th</u>

3. Do you know which sacred holiday in the spring changes dates? <u>le premier mai</u>

7 The Classroom

Claude's clue:

$$\left.\begin{array}{l} o \\ au \\ eau \end{array}\right\} = oh$$

rose, stylo   Claude, **au**jourd'hui   **beau, bureau**

Learn the names of the objects in your classroom.
See how many classroom objects you can remember at a time without having to look at the book:

un étudiant
un garçon

un cahier

un stylo

une table

une chaise

un livre

un tableau noir

une fenêtre

une porte

un morceau de craie

un professeur

une feuille de papier

une étudiante
une fille

un pupitre

un crayon

un bureau

In French, every noun is considered masculine or feminine. The masculine indefinite article (*a, an*) is **un**, and the feminine is **une**.

1. Name aloud as many of the classroom words in French as you can remember. Study the words you did not remember.

2. Write the name of the illustrations in French in the first column of blank lines.

3. Correct your work. Give yourself one point for each correct answer.

4. Now cover the illustrations and write the English meanings of the French words in the second column of blank lines.

5. Correct your work. Give yourself one point for each correct answer.

WRITE FRENCH WORDS HERE   WRITE ENGLISH WORDS HERE

1. _____   _____

2. _____   _____

3. _____   _____

4. _____   _____

5. _____   _____

6. _____   _____

WRITE FRENCH WORDS HERE   WRITE ENGLISH WORDS HERE

7. _____   _____

8. _____   _____

9. _____   _____

10. _____   _____

11. _____   _____

12. _____   _____

13. _____   _____

14. _____   _____

15. _____   _____

16. _____   _____

Thirty-two points is a perfect score. If you made a mistake, you can improve your score by repeating the exercise on a blank piece of paper and correcting it again.

Classroom Vocabulary Puzzle: To solve this puzzle, first express the following words in French then fit them in the puzzle vertically and horizontally:

5-letter words

chalk   __ __ __ __ __

girl   __ __ __ __ __

door   __ __ __ __ __

book   __ __ __ __ __

pen   __ __ __ __ __

table   __ __ __ __ __

6-letter words

chair   __ __ __ __ __ __

teacher's desk   __ __ __ __ __ __

notebook   __ __ __ __ __ __

paper   __ __ __ __ __ __

pencil   __ __ __ __ __ __

boy   __ __ __ __ __ __

7-letter words

window   __ __ __ __ __ __ __

student's desk   __ __ __ __ __ __ __

10-letter word

teacher   __ __ __ __ __ __ __ __ __ __

11-letter word combination

chalkboard   __ __ __ __ __ __ __ __ __ __ __

En France

School and Leisure Time

French school children have long school days and are also required to do at least one and a half to two hours of homework a day.

French family life is also very important, and parents tend to be strict.

PROGRAMME
Mai
et
Juin

Guitare classique : mardi : 19h-20h
Guitare folk : jeudi 17h -18h
Poterie : vendredi 17h-18h 30 (7 à 10ans)
        mercredi 17h -19h (11 à 14ans)
Peinture à l'huile : mercredi 18h - 20h
Danse moderne : lundi 17h -18h
Judo : mardi 18h - 19h
Atelier Théâtre : vendredi 17h-18h 30
Ordinateur : jeudi 17h-18h (7 à12ans)
        mardi 17h -19h (13 à16ans)

Because French schools normally do not sponsor activities like sports, dances, and games, most students go to youth centers in their neighborhoods. Here young people gather to attend classes in music, dance, drama, arts and crafts, photography, judo, computer science, fencing, soccer and other hobbies. Movies, plays, and weekend excursions are among the activities organized by the youth center.

1. Which sports, leisure activities, or classes are you involved in this year?

   _____

2. Where do you go for these activities? _____

   _____

3. Do you participate in group excursions? If yes, where did you go this year?

   _____

8 Colors

Claude's clue:

oi = wa

n**oi**r, tr**oi**s, madem**oi**selle

orange

jaune

vert

rouge

noir

bleu

brun

blanc   violet

rose

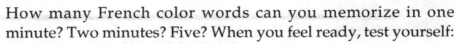

How many French color words can you memorize in one minute? Two minutes? Five? When you feel ready, test yourself:

1. Say as many French color words as you can remember.
2. Write the French color words in the first column of blank lines.
3. Check your work and give yourself one point for each correct answer.
4. Now cover the colors and write the English meanings of the French color words in the second column of blank lines.
5. Check your work and give yourself one point for each correct answer.

WRITE FRENCH WORDS HERE	WRITE ENGLISH WORDS HERE
1. rouge	red
2. orange	orange
3. jaune	yellow
4. vert	green
5. bleu	blue
6. viola	purple
7. rose	pink
8. blanche	white
9. maroon	brown
10. noir	black

Did you get 20 points? If not, try again with a blank piece of paper.

Here are pictures of items whose names you have already learned.

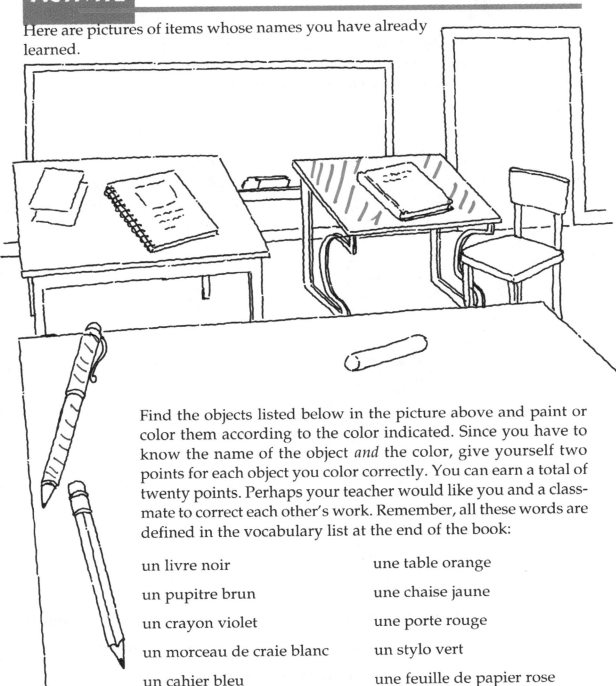

Find the objects listed below in the picture above and paint or color them according to the color indicated. Since you have to know the name of the object *and* the color, give yourself two points for each object you color correctly. You can earn a total of twenty points. Perhaps your teacher would like you and a classmate to correct each other's work. Remember, all these words are defined in the vocabulary list at the end of the book:

un livre noir

un pupitre brun

un crayon violet

un morceau de craie blanc

un cahier bleu

une table orange

une chaise jaune

une porte rouge

un stylo vert

une feuille de papier rose

You've already seen this map of the world. Color all the countries where French is spoken. Color the countries in each continent according to the colors below:

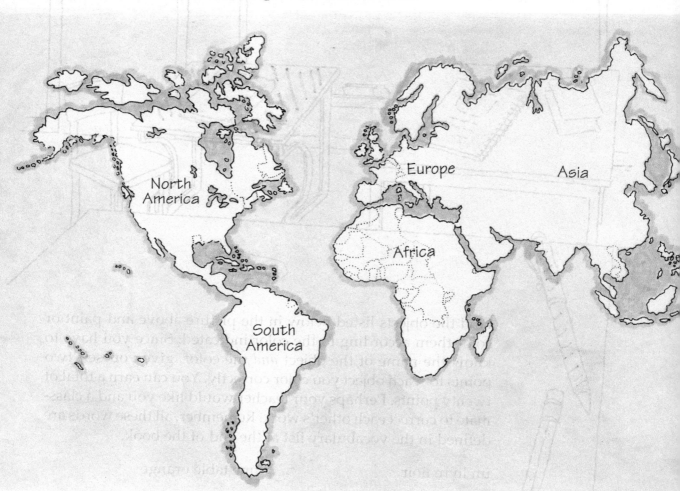

Europe — **jaune**   South America — **rouge**

Africa — **bleu**   North America — **vert**

Island Countries — **orange**

9 The Body

Claude's clue:

Final consonants are often not pronounced.

nez, pied, bras

la tête
l'œil
le nez
la bouche
la main
l'oreille
le bras
la jambe
le pied

When you want to talk about yourself in French, you will need to know the names of the parts of the body. Study them now. How many names can you remember without having to look at the book?

You have already learned that the masculine article **un** and the feminine article **une** mean *a, an*. Now let's learn how to express English *the*. Did you notice the words **le**, **la**, and **l'** before all of the nouns? To say *the*, French uses three words: **le** before masculine nouns that start with a consonant; **la** before feminine nouns that start with a consonant; and **l'** before masculine or feminine nouns that start with a vowel or with **h**.

ACTIVITÉ

Fill in the names of the parts of the body:

la tête

l'oreille

la bouche

l'oeil

la nez

la main

le bras

la jambe

le pied

ACTIVITÉ

Choose a partner. Point to each other's hand, foot, and so on, and ask, **"Qu'est-ce que c'est?"** Answer, **"C'est une main." "C'est un pied."** And so on.

Complete this crossword puzzle with the
French names of the parts of the body:

Across

Down

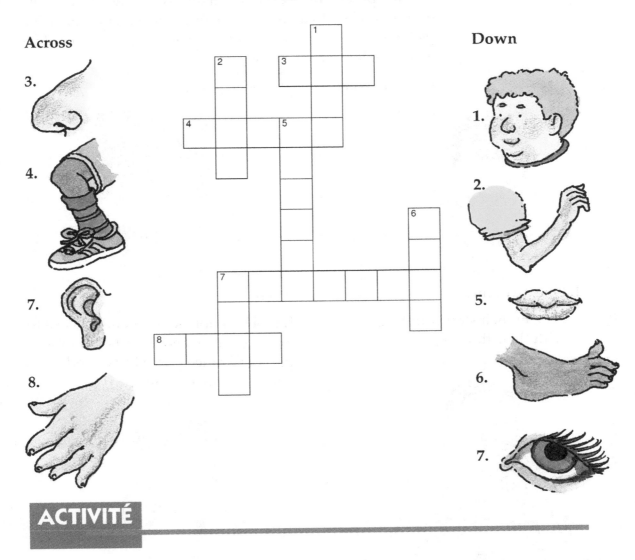

3.

4.

7.

8.

1.

2.

5.

6.

7.

"Simon dit" means *"Simon says."* Move or point to that part of
the body Simon refers to if you hear the words **"Simon dit."** If
you do not hear the words **"Simon dit,"** don't move at all.

Gestures

In every culture, gestures play an important role in communicating ideas and feelings. Gestures may be accompanied by a word or phrase. In most situations, however, the meaning of a gesture is clear to a native speaker or listener. Gestures, like pictures, are often more expressive than words and contribute to a more lively conversation.

Here are some typical French gestures:

1. One, two, three . . .

[The French start counting with their thumb.]

2. Hi!

[French people kiss on both cheeks to greet relatives and friends. In some parts of France, three kisses and even four are exchanged.]

3. Wonderful!

4. You must be kidding!

5. I've had it up to here.

6. Not a penny. Nothing!

7. You must be crazy!

8. I don't know.

1. Can you think of gestures Americans use to express their feelings or ideas?

_____

_____

2. What gestures do you use?_____

_____

_____

10 Talking About Yourself

Claude's clue:

When a word ends in **e**, the consonant before the **e** is pronounced.

fort forte   laid laide   gros grosse

An adjective describes a person, place, or thing. In the sentence "The beautiful girl is happy," *beautiful* and *happy* are adjectives that describe *girl*. Many adjectives are easy to remember if you think of them in pairs:

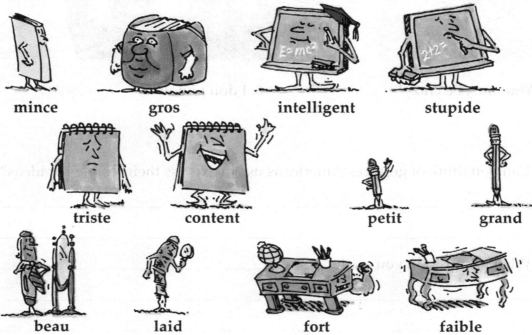

mince   gros   intelligent   stupide

triste   content   petit   grand

beau   laid   fort   faible

ACTIVITÉ

Cover page 50 with a sheet of paper and write on the lines below the French adjectives that describe the objects you see:

1. _____   2. _____   3. _____

4. _____   5. _____   6. _____

7. _____   8. _____   9. _____

10. _____   11. _____   12. _____

Dialog 3   *Je suis ...*

Let's take a closer look at some of the words you learned in Dialog 3:

Je suis . . .

Tu es . . .

Il est . . .
Le garçon est . . .

Elle est . . .
La fille est . . .

Look at the adjectives on the left that could describe a boy. Compare them with the adjectives on the right that could describe a girl:

content	contente
faible	faible
fort	forte
grand	grande
intelligent	intelligente
intéressant	intéressante
laid	laide
malheureux	malheureuse
petit	petite

French adjectives, like French nouns, have a gender. A feminine adjective is used to describe a feminine noun and a masculine adjective is used to describe a masculine noun. Which letter do we add to the masculine adjective to get the feminine? Some are the same. Note the change from *x* to *se* in malheureuse.

Use as many adjectives on page 55 as possible to describe these animals:

_____   _____

_____   _____

_____   _____

_____   _____

Now let's learn more about adjectives. After reading the explanations, fill in the blanks with the correct form of the adjective that describes the people and animals in the pictures:

1. You have already learned that when a word ends in é, like **enchanté**, adding an **e** creates the feminine form:

   Le garçon est _____.

   La fille est _____.

2. **Mince, stupide, triste**, and **faible** do not change in the feminine because they already end in **e**:

La fille est _____.

Le professeur est _____ aussi.

Le garçon est _____.

La fille est _____ aussi.

3. **Gros** becomes **grosse**:

Il est _____.

Elle est _____.

4. **Beau** becomes **belle**:

Le chat est _____.

La chatte est _____.

1. How many of the boys in this basketball team can you describe? Write the adjective from page 50 that best describes each player next to his number in the column of blank lines:

GARÇONS

1 _____
2 _____
3 _____
4 _____
5 _____
6 _____
7 _____
8 _____
9 _____
10 _____

2. How would you change the adjectives to describe each player of the girls' team? Write the adjective that best describes each player next to her number in the column of blank lines:

FILLES

1 _____

2 _____

3 _____

4 _____

5 _____

6 _____

7 _____

8 _____

9 _____

10 _____

59

ACTIVITÉ

Your teacher will now divide you into small groups to practice describing yourself and one another.

ACTIVITÉ

Play charades with the adjectives you have learned. Your teacher will divide the class into teams, and a member from one team will stand in front of the class and act out the various ways he or she would look if sad, intelligent, fat, and so on.

En France Sports

In France, soccer (**le football**) is the national sport. All of the larger French cities have home teams. Each team can be identified by the distinctive colors of its uniform. The best soccer teams compete for the national championship, and there are also international matches between the best professional soccer teams in Europe and in the world. On Sunday afternoons, amateurs play on soccer teams organized by groups of friends, clubs, companies, and municipalities.

Le Tour de France, which takes place annually in June and July, is the longest and best-known bicycle race in the world. 130 to 200 participants from many countries compete in this spectacular event, which lasts over a twenty-day period and covers more than 1,500 miles going through the Alps and the Pyrenees. Each year, a different French city is chosen as the starting point, with Paris always the final destination. The winner of the race receives a large sum of money, but, more importantly, becomes a national hero in his country.

1. Which sports are most popular in America? _____

_____

2. Which sports do you like to play, and which ones do you just like to watch?

_____

_____

11 Recycling French

Your teacher will now give you time to use your French. Think of all you have learned!

- You can say your name!
- You can count and do math!
- You can name the days of the week and the months of the year!
- You can name objects in the classroom with their colors!
- You can describe yourself and others and point out parts of the body!

When someone asks if you can speak French: **Parles-tu français?**, now you can answer: **Oui, je parle français!**

ACTIVITÉ

Fill in the boxes with the French meanings and you will find a mystery word in one of the longest vertical columns. Write the mystery word in French and English in the blanks provided:

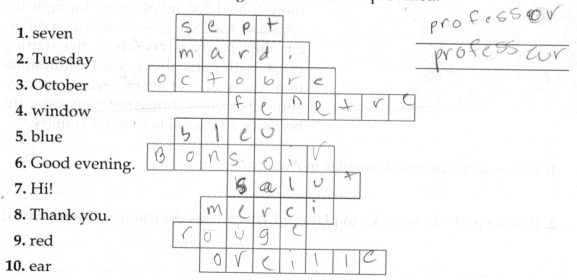

1. seven — s e p t
2. Tuesday — m a r d i
3. October — o c t o b r e
4. window — f e n e t r e
5. blue — b l e u
6. Good evening. — B o n s o i r
7. Hi! — s a l u t
8. Thank you. — m e r c i
9. red — r o u g e
10. ear — o r e i l l e

professor
professeur

Colors: What would this funny monster look like if you could color the parts of its body? Write the names of the numbered parts of the body and colors you would choose in the blanks below. Then color the parts of the body in the picture:

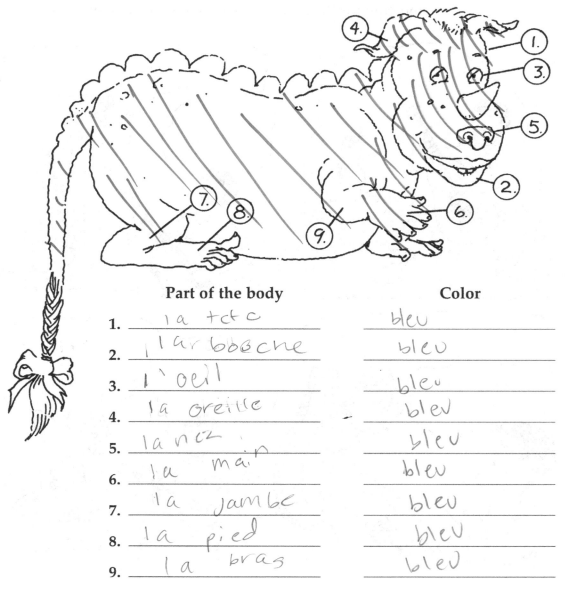

	Part of the body	**Color**
1.	la tête	bleu
2.	l'ar bôôche	bleu
3.	l'oeil	bleu
4.	la oreille	bleu
5.	la nez	bleu
6.	la main	bleu
7.	la jambe	bleu
8.	la pied	bleu
9.	la bras	bleu

ACTIVITÉ

Can you complete these dialogs or express the following ideas in French?

1. You overhear the conversation of these two people, who are meeting for the first time. Complete the dialog:

2. Peter is teaching some French words to his little brother. Complete the dialog:

3. What do you think these friends are saying to each other?

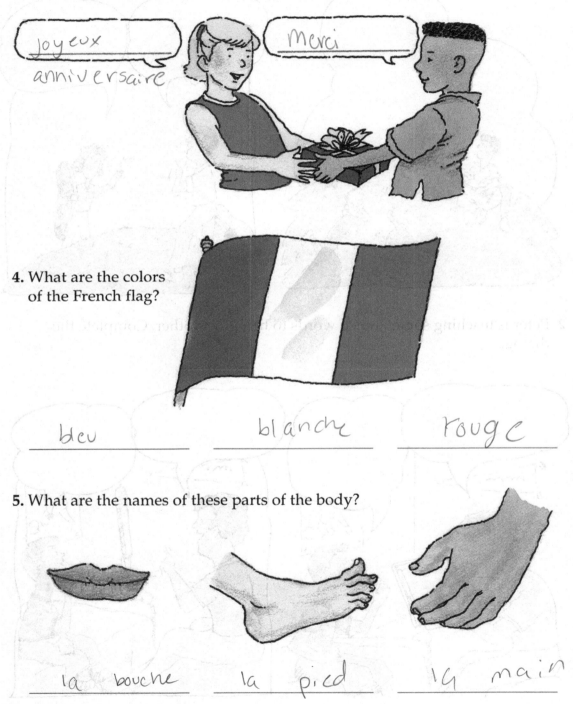

Joyeux anniversaire

Merci

4. What are the colors of the French flag?

bleu   blanche   rouge

5. What are the names of these parts of the body?

la bouche   la pied   la main

6. What days of the week are missing from this agenda?

7. What month is it?

avril

Jullict

becembre

8. What adjectives describe these young people?

contente

triste

forte

Loto is played like Bingo, except that our **Loto** game is played with words. Select French words from categories in the vocabulary list on pages 70 to 73 as directed by your teacher. Write one word across in each square at random from the chosen categories.

Your teacher will read the English meaning of the **Loto** words. If one of the French words on your card matches the English word you hear, mark that square with a small star. When you have five stars in a row, either horizontally, vertically, or diagonally, call out, **"J'ai gagné!"** (*"I won!"*)

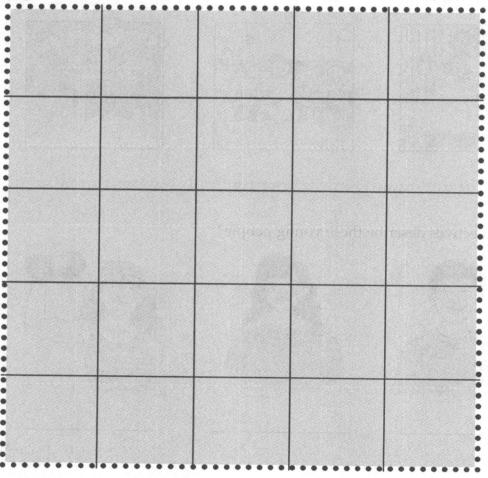

Vivent les différences! *(Hurrah for the differences!)*

Now that you have learned quite a bit about the French language and about France and its people, can you list the differences between French and American people that impressed you most? Jog your memory by looking over cultural pages 15, 23, 32–33, 40, 48–49, and 61.

An example is given to get you started:

FRENCH	AMERICAN
1. *Friends and relatives greet each other with kisses on both cheeks.*	*Friends and relatives say "Hi" and may kiss women on the cheek.*
2.	
3.	
4.	
5.	
6.	

Vocabulary

Numbers

un	1
deux	2
trois	3
quatre	4
cinq	5
six	6
sept	7
huit	8
neuf	9
dix	10
onze	11
douze	12
treize	13
quatorze	14
quinze	15
seize	16
dix-sept	17
dix-huit	18
dix-neuf	19
vingt	20
vingt et un	21
vingt-deux	22
vingt-trois	23
vingt-quatre	24
vingt-cinq	25
vingt-six	26
vingt-sept	27
vingt-huit	28
vingt-neuf	29
trente	30
trente et un	31
trente-deux	32
trente-trois	33
trente-quatre	34
trente-cinq	35
trente-six	36
trente-sept	37
trente-huit	38
trente-neuf	39
quarante	40

Arithmetic

combien?	how many?
et	plus
font	equal
moins	minus

Days of the week

lundi	Monday
mardi	Tuesday
mercredi	Wednesday
jeudi	Thursday
vendredi	Friday
samedi	Saturday
dimanche	Sunday

Months of the year

janvier	January
février	February
mars	March
avril	April
mai	May
juin	June
juillet	July
août	August
septembre	September
octobre	October
novembre	November
décembre	December

The Classroom

un bureau	a (teacher's) desk
un cahier	a notebook
une chaise	a chair
un crayon	a pencil
un étudiant	a (male) student
une étudiante	a (female) student
une fenêtre	a window
une feuille de papier	a sheet of paper
une fille	a girl
un garçon	a boy
un livre	a book
un morceau de craie	a piece of chalk
une porte	a door
un professeur	a teacher
un pupitre	a (student's) desk
un stylo	a ballpoint pen
une table	a table
un tableau noir	a chalkboard

Colors

blanc, blanche	white
bleu, bleue	blue
brun, brune	brown
jaune	yellow
noir, noire	black
orange	orange
rose	pink
rouge	red
vert, verte	green
violet, violette	purple

The Body

la bouche	the mouth
le bras	the arm
la jambe	the leg
la main	the hand
le nez	the nose
l'œil	the eye
l'oreille	the ear
le pied	the foot
la tête	the head

Adjectives

beau, belle	handsome, beautiful
content, contente	happy
enchanté, enchantée	pleased to meet you
faible	weak
fort, forte	strong
grand, grande	tall
gros, grosse	fat
intelligent, intelligente	intelligent
intéressant, intéressante	interesting
laid, laide	ugly
malheureux, malheureuse	unhappy
mince	thin
petit, petite	short, small
stupide	stupid
triste	sad

Expressions and phrases

Comment t'appelles-tu?	What's your name?
Je m'appelle . . .	My name is . . .
Enchanté(e).	Pleased to meet you.
Ça va?	How's it going?
Ça va bien.	Everything's fine.
Comme ci, comme ça.	So, so.
Et toi?	And you?
C'est aujourd'hui . . .	Today is . . .
Mon Anniversaire est . . .	My birthday is . . .
Qu' est-ce que c' est?	What is it? / What's that?
C' est . . .	It is . . . / That is . . .
Pour toi.	For you.
Bonjour.	Hello.
Salut!	Hi!
Au revoir.	Good-bye. See you.
Je suis . . .	I am . . .
Tu es . . .	You are . . .
Il est . . .	He is . . .

Elle est . . .	She is . . .
La fille est . . .	The girl is . . .
Le garçon est . . .	The boy is . . .
Es-tu . . .?	Are you . . .?
Merci (beaucoup).	Thank you (very much).
De rien.	You're welcome.
Parles-tu français?	Do you speak French?
Je parle français.	I speak French.
J'ai gagné.	I won.
Oui.	Yes.
Non.	No.
monsieur	Mister, sir
mademoiselle	Miss
madame	madam, Mrs.
aussi	also
et	and
le chat	the (male) cat
la chatte	the (female) cat
le premier	the first
maintenant	now
pourquoi?	why?
parce que	because
un soda	carbonated fruit drink
très	very